A Simple HR Story

FROM SIPPING COFFEE TO BREWING CAREERS

SANKETH RAMKRISHNAMURTHY

Copyright © 2025 by Sanketh Ramkrishnamurthy

All rights reserved.

This book or any portion thereof may not be reproduced or used in any manner whatsoever without the express written permission of the respective writer of the respective content except for the use of brief quotations in a book review.

The writer of the respective work holds sole responsibility for the originality of the content and IndiePress is not responsible in any way whatsoever.

Printed in India

IndiePress

ISBN: 978-93-7197-162-1

First Printing, 2025

IndiePress

A division of Nasadiya Technologies Private Ltd.

Koramangala, Bengaluru

Karnataka-560029

http://indiepress.in/

Edited by MAP Systems, Bengaluru

Typeset by MAP Systems, Bengaluru

Book Cover designed by Nikhil Kamath

Publishing Consultant: Shrey Saboo

Contents

Preface		vii
Chapter 1:	The Journey Begins	1
Chapter 2:	Hiring Smarter, Not Just Faster	9
Chapter 3:	When Happy Employees Brew Success	17
Chapter 4:	Learning & Development–Brewing Growth, One Sip at a Time	23
Chapter 5:	Performance Management–More Than Just Annual Reviews	29
Chapter 6:	Brewing Tough Conversations	35
Chapter 7:	HR Technology–Work Smarter, Not Harder	43
Chapter 8:	The Cost of Poor HR–Compliance and Risk Management	49
Chapter 9:	Retention–The Secret Weapon for Profitability	57
Chapter 10:	Work-Life Balance–Brewing Happiness Beyond the Office	63

Chapter 11: HR's Seat at the Table—Becoming a
Business Partner   69

Chapter 12: Beyond Management—Brewing a Legacy of
Leadership   77

Chapter 13: Brewing Collaboration—Conflict Resolution
in Product Engineering   83

Chapter 14: Brewing Future Leaders—Succession
Planning and Career Growth   87

Chapter 15: The Final Promotion—Becoming CHRO   95

Chapter 16: The Future of Profitable HR—Brewing
Beyond the Present   101

Conclusion   107

Acknowledgements   113

About the Author   117

Preface

Arjun took a slow, thoughtful sip of his coffee, staring out at the city skyline—lost in thought. The steam curled up from the cup, mingling with the cool morning air, yet the warmth did little to ease the cold knot of worry in his chest. His company was facing a hiring crisis—not merely a shortage of CVs, but a deeper issue gnawing at the very foundation of the business. Great talent was out there, but something felt broken. The disconnect between HR and business goals was widening—no matter how many late nights he spent strategising, the gap seemed impossible to bridge.

He had always thought of HR as a straightforward function: hiring, policies, and payroll. Lately, every hire felt like a gamble; every policy seemed to miss the mark; the once-structured world of HR now felt like a maze with shifting walls. Employees were disengaged. Turnover was rising. Leaders wanted results, not excuses. The weight of expectations pressed heavily on his shoulders, and in that quiet moment—with a steaming cup in hand—the realisation struck him like the first jolt of caffeine:

HR wasn't just about filling positions; it was about crafting careers. It was about creating an environment where people didn't just work—they flourished.

Just like the perfect brew, HR requires the right blend, patience and an understanding of its essential elements.

Welcome to *A Simple HR Story*—a journey of professional and personal transformation. This isn't just another book about HR strategies or best practices—it's a journey. It is the story of how a small-town dreamer, Arjun, stepped into the world of HR—filled with ambition but little understanding of its true power. He started as an eager HR professional, diligently following processes, enforcing policies, and ticking boxes. But as he faced hiring dilemmas, disengaged employees, and leadership challenges, he realised that HR was so much more than spreadsheets and procedures. HR isn't about paperwork—it's about people. HR isn't about rules—it's about relationships.

Through Arjun's experiences, you'll witness how he reimagines hiring, fosters a culture of continuous learning, and harnesses technology to redefine HR's role in business success. You'll experience his frustrations, his triumphs, and his moments of clarity as he discovers that HR isn't just a function—it's the heartbeat of every thriving organisation.

Little did Arjun know that one day, he would stand in the boardroom—not merely defending HR's role but proving its power as a strategic force capable of shaping the company's future.

Whether you're an aspiring HR professional or a seasoned leader, Arjun's journey will resonate with you:

If you're just starting out in HR, you'll navigate real-world challenges through Arjun's eyes, gaining confidence to shape meaningful workplace experiences.

If you're a seasoned leader, Arjun's transformation will reignite your passion for people-focused leadership, offering fresh perspectives and innovative strategies.

If you're a student or an aspiring HR professional, this book will bridge the gap between theory and practice, by providing practical insights into the dynamic world of HR.

If you're an entrepreneur or business leader, you'll see how HR, when done well, is a powerful strategic partner in driving organisational success.

Just like the perfect coffee blend, great HR isn't created overnight—it's crafted with thought, care, and continuous refinement.

By the time you finish this book, you'll have the tools to:

Transform conventional HR practices into strategic initiatives. Use empathy, innovation, and resilience to drive organisational success. Manage talent effectively, foster engagement, and build a thriving culture. Utilise technology and data-driven approaches for more informed decision-making. Embrace personal growth and adaptability as essential to professional excellence.

As you turn these pages, grab your favourite cup of coffee and step into Arjun's world—a world where HR is not merely a department, but a craft. A craft that, when brewed with care, transforms workplaces, empowers people, and shapes the future.

Let's begin brewing.

Chapter 1

The Journey Begins
From Sipping Coffee to Brewing Careers

The aroma of instant coffee curled through the dimly lit room, blending with the musky scent of damp earth drifting in from the open window. Arjun sat at the edge of his bed, cradling a steaming cup, his gaze lost in the rising swirls. The city still slumbered, but his thoughts were wide awake.

Today wasn't just another day—it was the first sip of a new beginning.

His fingers brushed the frayed edges of a folded note tucked inside his wallet. The ink had faded, but the words still burned bright in his mind:

Education is your path—never stop learning.

These words had seen him through rejection letters, failed interviews, and sleepless nights spent clinging to hope and cheap coffee.

Arjun had once stumbled into an internship at a local NGO, hoping to get a feel for corporate life. But instead of structured roles, he found chaos. There was no induction, no mentor—only spreadsheets dumped on his desk and vague instructions. That experience had left him feeling like an outsider, and the self-doubt had taken root. He often questioned whether he was cut out for the world of HR.

He zipped up his battered backpack and glanced at his roommates, still asleep. Their cramped room had been more than shelter; it had been their sanctuary. Over shared dreams and instant coffee, they had become more than friends—they were survivors.

But today, Arjun wasn't just dreaming. He was stepping into his future. His first job at Aditya Solutions awaited.

A First Sip of Success

The bus jolted forward, plunging Arjun into the heart of Bangalore's morning buzz. Street vendors opened shop, corporate towers glinted under a golden sun, and young professionals hustled by with intent.

For years, he had watched this world from the sidelines. Today, he was part of it.

As the bus halted, the towering facade of Aditya Solutions loomed ahead. The glass reflected his hesitant image. He clutched his offer letter tighter and stepped forward.

"Welcome to Aditya Solutions," a warm voice greeted. Meera, the HR executive, handed him a visitor badge with a kind smile. A small gesture, but to Arjun, it felt monumental.

Inside, the air buzzed with energy—the hum of conversations, the rhythm of keyboards, the purposeful footsteps of ambition. Arjun felt his heart race—not with fear, but with anticipation.

Still, the jitters of being a fresher clung to him. Every smiling face seemed more confident, every hallway more daunting. He fumbled with his bag, accidentally dropped his ID, and even entered the wrong meeting room. But instead of ridicule, he was met with laughter, gentle corrections, and welcoming smiles.

The first week was a whirlwind of induction sessions, HRMS logins, policy handbooks, and tea breaks. Arjun was introduced to the team gradually. He shadowed Meera and Ravi through various meetings, quietly observing how employee queries were handled and how decisions were made. He jotted down everything in a small, dog-eared notebook—each term, each acronym, each process.

There were moments of confusion. Once, he forgot to respond to an important onboarding email, and Ravi gently pointed out the importance of timelines. Another time, he sat frozen during a meeting, unable to answer a simple question about the leave policy. Embarrassed, he spent the next weekend poring over the employee manual.

Yet, despite the glitches, something within him shifted. He realised learning wasn't about knowing everything on Day One—it was about being curious and resilient.

Then came a voice that would define his journey.

"Come, Arjun. Let's get started." Mr. Ravi, his mentor, stood tall—greying hair, wise eyes, and the calm assurance of a man who had weathered storms.

Arjun followed, clutching his coffee like a shield.

From Coffee Breaks to Career Builders

His first real task came a couple of weeks later: assist with employee onboarding. But as Ravi guided him through the process, Arjun discovered it was far more than forms and checklists.

"First impressions shape an entire journey," Ravi explained as they welcomed a batch of new hires. "A great onboarding experience is like the first sip of coffee—it sets the tone for what's to come."

Determined to shine, Arjun led an orientation for Rahul, one of the new employees. He rushed through the material, ticking off points with mechanical precision. His goal was completion, not connection.

At lunch, Arjun noticed Rahul sitting alone, staring blankly at the handbook. Something tugged at him.

"Hey, how's it going?" Arjun asked.

Rahul looked up, unsure. "Honestly? I feel lost. I barely remember anything. I don't know who to ask for help."

Arjun's stomach sank. He had delivered information but failed to make Rahul feel welcome.

That evening, Ravi pulled him aside. "You rushed it, didn't you?"

Arjun sighed. "I thought I was doing it right... but I just overwhelmed him."

Ravi smiled, placing a hand on his shoulder. "Onboarding isn't about dumping data. It's about building connection. Help them feel at home first, and the learning will follow."

The next day, Arjun sat with Rahul at lunch, introduced him around, and made sure he knew whom to approach. Over time, Rahul's confidence grew—and so did Arjun's understanding.

Lesson 1: Onboarding isn't a formality; it's the first chapter of someone's story.

Steaming Challenges, Stirring Solutions

Weeks flowed by like steam from a morning brew. Arjun was no longer the wide-eyed newcomer—he was finding rhythm in the pulse of HR.

Then came the real test.

One afternoon, the office erupted. Sandeep, a frustrated employee, barged into HR, demanding a role change. His words were edged with anger, his judgment clouded.

Arjun stood frozen, unsure. Ravi opened his office door and gestured to him. Inside, the calm returned. "This isn't about blame, Arjun," Ravi said softly. "It's about listening. Go ahead."

As Sandeep vented, Arjun listened. He said little, just nodded, creating space. Slowly, the anger gave way to rawness. They didn't resolve everything, but when Sandeep left, he was calmer and open to next steps.

Lesson 2: Empathy is the bridge between misunderstanding and resolution.

That evening, sipping chai, Arjun turned to Ravi. "I always thought HR was just about policies. But it's more, isn't it?"

Ravi nodded. "HR isn't about managing people. It's about helping them grow. Every challenge, every new hire—you have the power to shape careers, Arjun."

Lesson 3: True leadership in HR isn't about controlling people; it's about empowering them.

Final Reflection

- Onboarding is the foundation of an employee's journey—make it meaningful.

- Empathy isn't optional in HR; it's the glue that holds teams together.

- Feedback isn't just about improvement; it's about inspiring growth.

- HR isn't about processes—it's about people.

Self-Written Quote: *HR isn't just a department—it's the art of brewing success, one person at a time.*

Self-Written Formula: *People + Purpose + Patience = Productive HR*

Under the glow of the city's streetlights, Arjun walked home, his notebook filled with lessons he never imagined. The journey was no longer about surviving.

It was about making an impact. And he was just getting started.

Chapter 2

Hiring Smarter, Not Just Faster
From Sipping Coffee to Brewing Careers

Arjun's second month at Aditya Solutions marked a turning point. What had once been a steady rhythm in HR had evolved into a fast-paced frenzy. The hiring dashboard blinked with open roles like warning lights—urgent, demanding, unyielding. Twenty hires. One month. No room for mistakes. Every hallway conversation echoed with the same underlying pressure: speed was key.

Arjun leaned back in his chair, slowly sipping his coffee. The world outside the HR department might have seen them relaxing between tasks, but it never noticed the invisible weight that came with the role. Hiring wasn't about filling seats—it was about finding the right blend: skills, culture, potential. His coffee today wasn't just a drink; it was fuel for the mission ahead.

The Hiring Challenge: Brewing Under Pressure – 20 Days, 20 Hires

The clock ticked as Arjun reviewed the updated recruitment plan Mr. Ravi handed him.

"We need twenty hires by month-end," Ravi said, matter-of-fact. "Fast. Smart. No room for mistakes."

The weight settled on Arjun. His instinct urged speed—process applications, schedule interviews, meet the target. But when he saw the towering pile of résumés, his father's words surfaced: "Do it with heart and patience."

Rushing through hiring was like making coffee without letting it brew—bitter, ineffective, and disappointing. Speed was critical. But quality? Non-negotiable. He needed a system that ensured both.

Then came the email:

URGENT: Five Software Engineers Needed in 10 Days.

Manoj, the software division's hiring manager, had escalated the urgency. A new client project had kicked off, and missing these hires meant missing deadlines.

The next morning, Ravi called him in.

"We don't have time for perfection, Arjun," he said. "Just fill the roles."

Arjun stayed calm. "Speed matters, Ravi. But hiring the wrong people costs us more. We need both speed and accuracy."

Ravi sighed. "Last time we rushed, we hired Sameer. Stellar résumé, good experience—but six weeks in, he couldn't keep up. Slowed the team down. We let him go."

Arjun nodded. He remembered.

"I don't want another Sameer," Ravi added. "But we can't wait forever. The client is watching."

"Exactly," Arjun said. "That's why we need to hire smart, not just fast. Like brewing the perfect cup: right beans, right process, just enough time."

Ravi narrowed his eyes. "Fine. Show me a better way."

And so, the real challenge began.

A Candidate's Doubt, A Recruiter's Responsibility – Choosing the Right Blend

Among the résumés, one application stood out: Karthik Reddy. Strong technical skills, limited experience. But his cover letter struck a chord:

"I may not have the experience of others, but I learn fast. I just need someone to believe in me."

Arjun scheduled an interview. Karthik's problem-solving was promising, but his lack of exposure made Manoj hesitant.

"He's good, but we have stronger candidates," Manoj said, exasperated. "We can't afford risks."

That evening, Arjun sought advice from Sunita, a seasoned HR leader.

"Hiring isn't about ticking boxes," she said, stirring her chai. "The best hires aren't always the most experienced—they're the ones who want to grow. Someone has to take a chance on them."

Encouraged, Arjun invited Karthik for an informal chat. This time, his passion shone. He spoke of self-led projects, his drive to learn.

Just as Arjun felt confident, a new profile landed: Rohan Shetty. Highly experienced, technically sound. But something felt off. His responses were rigid. Adaptability? Missing.

The Tough Decision – Bold Choices Make the Best Brews

Late one evening, Arjun sat in his office, torn. Rohan was the safer bet—immediate impact, minimal risk. Karthik? A gamble.

What if I'm wrong? he wondered. *What if Karthik struggles?*

Doubt lingered. But hiring wasn't about easy choices—it was about trust, growth, and standing by your call.

The next morning, Arjun approached Ravi.

"I'm recommending Karthik for the role."

Ravi raised an eyebrow. "Are you sure? We're already behind."

"We need someone who can grow with us," Arjun said firmly.

Ravi paused, then nodded slowly. "Fine. But this better work out."

Two days later, Karthik was hired.

The Brew in Progress – 60 Days Later

Two months in, Arjun often found himself watching Karthik at the engineering bay—notebook in hand, questions flying, soaking in knowledge like a sponge in warm water.

But it wasn't all smooth.

In week two, Karthik submitted a module missing key edge cases—a near-miss for a client demo. Manoj frowned. "This is what I was worried about."

Arjun didn't flinch. He arranged a joint review with Karthik and senior engineer Nandita—not to criticize, but to coach.

"Think of this like adjusting the grind size," Arjun said over a debrief coffee. "Your beans are great, but the brew's not consistent yet. With time and mentoring, it will be."

Karthik nodded, embarrassed but eager. "Thanks for not giving up on me."

In the following weeks:
- He stayed late, shadowing seniors.
- He initiated his own stand-up notes.
- He volunteered to mentor an intern to test his understanding.

By Day 60, he owned a module end-to-end. Manoj left a note:

"Good work. You've come a long way."

Later that day, Karthik left an envelope on Arjun's desk. Inside was a single coffee bean, wrapped in tissue. The note read:

"Still brewing—but thank you for the roast."

Arjun chuckled, holding the note like a trophy. Sometimes, it wasn't the instant espresso that left a mark—it was the slow pour-over, rich in patience and promise.

Final Reflection – Brewing Beyond the Offer Letter

That night, Arjun turned to his journal with a renewed insight. Hiring didn't end with an offer letter. The real brew began on Day One, and needed care through the first few sips.

He scribbled a new line beneath his earlier formula:

"Hiring doesn't end with selection—it begins with integration. The right environment turns potential into performance."

Right Skills + Cultural Fit + Business Need = The Perfect Brew (Successful Hire)

He'd made a bold choice. It paid off. But something told him: the bigger challenges were still ahead.

Self-Written Quote:

"Hiring isn't about filling roles—it's about recognising potential. Just like coffee, great hires take time to brew, and the best ones leave a lasting impact."

As he took the last sip of his coffee, Arjun smiled.

HR wasn't about sipping coffee. It was about brewing futures— one carefully nurtured potential at a time.

Chapter 3

When Happy Employees Brew Success

Arjun's first few weeks at the company were a caffeine-fueled blur of onboarding sessions and strategy decks. Yet between the swirl of activity he sensed a faint bitterness in the aftertaste. Employee engagement, he realised, couldn't be sweetened with free lattes alone; it had to be brewed slowly, with intention. **He needed more than sugar and spice—it was time to start brewing something deeper.**

The First Signs: A Lukewarm Workplace

The realisation came in gentle drips. Fewer volunteers for stretch projects. Shorter hallway chats. Laughter that once bubbled like fresh espresso now sounded like reheated drip.

One afternoon Arjun passed **Neha's** desk—the creative spark behind *Campaign Phoenix*, the marketing push that revived an entire product line. She was the last to leave on most nights, ideas streaming faster than the office Wi-Fi. Today she was slipping her laptop into her bag before sunset.

"Heading out already?" Arjun asked.

Neha managed a smile, eyes on the floor. "Just… feeling a bit drained."

It looked small, almost invisible. But the next day it repeated, and the next. The spark in Neha's eyes dimmed to embers.

The Email That Stung

Three days later Arjun's inbox chimed:

Subject: Resignation Letter – Neha R.

His stomach tightened—no dramatic punch, just a cold trickle of dread. Neha was the fifth high-potential employee in two weeks. Raghav, the veteran developer; Pooja, the client whisperer; Amit and Sonia, rising stars—all gone or going.

The office felt like coffee left on the countertop—lukewarm and somehow sad.

The Failed Engagement Experiment

Panicked, Arjun brewed up **"Fun Fridays."** Games, snacks, a DJ spinning lo-fi beats for an hour.

The result? Smiles that flickered like weak sparks. A few employees slipped out early, others hovered at the edge of the room counting minutes. Arjun tasted the hollow sweetness of a syrupy drink—nice on the surface, empty underneath.

Doubt—and a Dash of Pushback

At the next leadership stand-up he floated bolder ideas: mentorships, career pathways, recognition rituals.

"Mentorships take time," one manager sighed.

"We have products to ship," another added.

Arjun hesitated, the aroma of self-doubt rising. Then he steadied the cup in his hands.

"So does hiring five new Nehas," he said quietly.

Silence settled, thick as a dark roast. The room moved on, but the seed was planted.

Neha's Final Sip

Before her last day, Arjun invited Neha for coffee. Steam curled between them like unsaid words.

"Be honest," he asked. "Why are you really leaving?"

Neha stirred her cup, watching the swirl.

"I didn't leave for a higher salary," she said. "I left because I stopped feeling like I mattered. I wanted a promotion, a map for my growth... but no one asked."

Her words hit like a sharp espresso shot—strong, undeniable.

Retention wasn't about counter-offers. It was about culture.

The Retention Brew: Stirring Up Change

Arjun launched a **Retention Revolution**, built on four core ingredients:

1. **The Mentorship Brew – Richer, Stronger Connections**

    Employees were paired with senior leaders who listened first and guided second. Raghav, who once felt invisible, now met weekly with the CTO; his code commits spoke of rediscovered passion.

2. **Custom Career Pathways – Brewing Growth**

    Structured growth discussions mapped clear futures. Priya, a mid-level developer, saw a roadmap and found fresh momentum.

3. **Real-Time Recognition – Freshly Brewed Appreciation**

    A culture of immediate shout-outs ensured effort never went stale. Sunil beamed when applauded in the daily huddle; confidence poured into his work.

4. **Open Conversations – Stronger Coffee, Stronger Bonds**

    Coffee with Leadership sessions opened valves of trust. Pooja voiced concerns about her role; leadership adjusted, and she decided to stay.

From Retention to Belonging

Within months the aroma changed. In a town-hall, a junior engineer stood and said,

"I used to think no one noticed my work. Now—I feel like I belong."

Applause thundered like beans cascading into a roaster.

Retention, Arjun realised, wasn't about holding on. It was about crafting a place people chose, day after day.

Final Reflection: Brewing Long-Term Success

Arjun took a slow, satisfied sip. The workplace was no longer lukewarm. It was alive—rich, strong, and energising.

> *"Engaged employees are like a well-brewed coffee—full-bodied and invigorating. Invest in them, and they don't just stay; they thrive."*

Lessons from Arjun's Journey – The Perfect Blend for Retention

1. Retention isn't about counter-offers—it's about culture.
2. Small signs of disengagement are early warnings—listen to the drips.
3. Employees leave when they don't see growth—mentorship and pathways are key.
4. Recognition isn't a luxury—it's motivation's fuel.
5. Leadership should be approachable—conversations build trust.

Formula: Recognition + Growth Opportunities + Leadership Trust = Happy, Productive Employees

As Arjun took his last sip of coffee, he smiled. The workplace was no longer lukewarm. It was brewing with energy, purpose, and passion. And that was the real win.

HR wasn't just about sipping coffee—it was about **brewing success—one engaged employee at a time.**

Chapter 4

Learning & Development–Brewing Growth, One Sip at a Time

The Morning Ritual

Every dawn, Arjun ground his coffee beans with deliberate care—not merely to wake himself, but to ponder growth. **Great coffee, like great learning, demands three things:**

- **The right beans** – fresh knowledge
- **The perfect water** – hands-on practice
- **Patience with heat & time** – reflection that unlocks depth

Yet even the finest blend can turn bitter if served poorly. Arjun learned that lesson the hard way.

When the Brew Went Cold

His first grand training initiative looked flawless on paper: celebrity trainers, polished slide decks, glossy handouts. Within two weeks, the classroom was emptier than the pantry at 6 p.m. Only three people showed up to the third session—and one slipped out halfway, steaming with frustration.

"I'd rather queue for this lukewarm machine coffee," someone joked at the vending machine. The words scalded more than the coffee ever could.

The CFO, Rajan, added heat: "We've poured thousands into this. Where's the aroma of ROI?"

That night Arjun sat over a cold, untouched cup, confidence unraveling faster than an abandoned brew. Sunita, the silver-haired HR sage, placed a fresh mug beside him.

"Looks like your coffee—and your training—went cold," she said. "Maybe it's not what you're pouring in, but **how** you're serving it."

The seed of reinvention was planted.

An Extra Dash of Doubt

The next morning, even *before* he could prototype a new approach, Meera—the skeptical Head of Operations—cornered him:

"A storytelling onboarding? Cross-functional barista days? Sounds frothy. Convince me this isn't just latte art."

Challenge accepted.

Listening First, Leading Second

Arjun swapped lecterns for listening posts. Coffee in hand, he roamed corridors, cafés, and Slack threads, brewing insight in real time.

Micro-Story 1: The New Joiner Who Didn't Know the 'Why' Aanya confessed during onboarding, "I still don't know *why* we exist." Arjun rebuilt onboarding as a story quest—new hires met customers, traced value chains, and pinned their role on a giant wall mural called **The Learning Trail**.

Micro-Story 2: The Quiet Developer Who Wanted to Speak Vinay, a brilliant coder, whispered, "Presenting? That's not me." Arjun paired him with Maya from Marketing. Six weeks later Vinay demo-ed a product roadmap to clients—voice steady, eyes bright.

Micro-Story 3: The HR Manager Who Feared Tech Numbers spooked Neha. Weekly **Skill-Labs** let her experiment without judgment. By quarter's end she dazzled leadership with an attrition dashboard.

A final nudge came when a spontaneous **'Latte & Learn' circle** popped up in the pantry—employees self-organising to share what they'd just discovered. Learning was no longer a mandate; it was a *movement*.

From Lecture to Lifestyle

To convert sparks into system, Arjun brewed five house specials:

1. **Immersive Onboarding** – customer calls, leader shadowing, and story maps.
2. **Employee-Driven Skill Votes** – like choosing a favourite roast each quarter.
3. **Role-Reversal Days** – engineers in empathy labs, HR in code debug rooms.
4. **Mentorship Roastery** – pairing novices with seasoned baristas of craft.
5. **Coffee Huddles** – 15-minute Friday reflections; no PowerPoints, just conversation.

Even Meera thawed when her team reduced onboarding time by 40% and cut defects on new projects.

Transforming Rohan – From Weak Brew to Bold Roast

Once labelled under-extracted talent, Rohan admitted, "I want to do better. I just don't know *how*."

Instead of another performance roast, Arjun placed him in the **Mentorship Programme** alongside Priya from Customer Success. Through live role-plays, shadowed calls, and reflective journaling, Rohan's flavour profile blossomed. Three months later his client satisfaction scores topped the chart.

"You didn't just train me," he told Arjun. "You believed in me. That changed the blend."

The G.R.O.W. Framework – Brewing at Scale

Letter	What It Means	A Quick Brew-In-Action
G – Goal Setting	Align personal and business goals	Neha set a SMART goal: "Automate attrition insights by Q3."
R – Resource Allocation	Access to courses, mentors, peer circles	She enrolled in a Coursera data course and booked weekly mentor shots with Rahul.
O – Opportunities to Practise	Mini-projects & hackathons	Led a micro-project analysing exit interviews, presenting findings over a "Data Macchiato" session.
W – Weekly Reflections	Debrief in Coffee Huddles	Shared wins & misses every Friday, refining her recipe.

Within six months, attrition dashboards became as routine as the morning espresso.

The Perfect Brew

- **25 %** rise in internal mobility
- **40 %** drop in onboarding time
- Record-high engagement scores

As Arjun locked up the office one evening, he cradled a steaming cup, caramel notes swirling. He realised he hadn't built a training programme—he'd *brewed transformation.*

"Learning is like coffee," he mused. "Intentional, patient, and best served the way people love to drink it. Brew it right, and they'll always come back for another sip."

Sunita clinked her mug to his. "Told you," she smiled. "Serve it warm, and the aroma does the rest."

Arjun's Brew Formula

Engaging Learning + Practice + Human Connection = A Thriving Workforce

Because HR isn't just about sipping coffee—it's about **brewing careers** with warmth, courage, and curiosity.

Chapter 5

Performance Management—More Than Just Annual Reviews

Feedback: The Steam That Keeps Growth Flowing

Arjun firmly believed that feedback is the key ingredient of growth. Much like a perfectly brewed cup of coffee, development needs the right balance of **boldness** and **warmth**—strong enough to spark improvement yet gentle enough to build confidence. In too many organisations, however, feedback is treated like **instant coffee**—hurried, impersonal, and served just once a year. If coffee tastes best when fresh, Arjun wondered, **why were companies waiting twelve months to tell employees how they were performing?**

> *"Annual performance reviews are outdated,"* he told his leadership team. *"If feedback is the key to improvement, why are we unlocking the door only once a year?"*

He set out to change that mindset at Aditya Solutions, determined to brew a culture of **continuous growth** rather than annual evaluation.

The Problem with Traditional Feedback — A Stale Brew

It began with **Rohan**, a talented yet struggling product designer. During a routine yearly review, Rohan sat opposite his manager, drumming anxious fingers on the table.

"Rohan, your designs haven't met the mark this quarter," the manager said, flipping through a stack of **dog-eared** review sheets.

Rohan's brow furrowed. *"No one mentioned that earlier. Had I known, I'd have fixed it months ago."*

"Well," the manager sighed, *"that's why we're telling you now. Focus on improving next year."*

Arjun, observing the exchange, watched frustration rise beneath the surface. The feedback was **late, vague, and unusable**—like sipping stale coffee: bitter, disappointing, and anything but energising.

That moment cemented his resolve: **No more outdated annual reviews.** Feedback would become *continuous, constructive, and collaborative* so employees could act immediately.

Pushback to Feedback — A Bitter First Sip

Not everyone welcomed the change. **Priya**, a senior developer, had long been defensive about criticism. During her first weekly check-in, her shoulders stiffened the instant feedback touched on code-quality gaps.

> *"I don't think anything is wrong with my work,"* Priya snapped, arms crossed. *"I've coded this way for years, and no one complained."*

Arjun paused; pushing too hard would only deepen resistance. He inhaled, then began with genuine appreciation.

> "Priya, your commitment to deadlines is outstanding, and the team counts on your expertise."

Her posture eased.

> "That said, there's always room to grow. Let's review two recent projects where we can boost efficiency together."

By starting with recognition and framing feedback as *shared growth*, Arjun turned Priya's resistance into curiosity. Over the next few weeks she experimented with new practices—and something unexpected happened.

A month later, Arjun overheard Priya encouraging a junior engineer:

"Your logic is solid, and I love how clean your tests are," she said. *"If you add a small performance benchmark, it'll shine even brighter. Let's pair tomorrow."*

Arjun smiled. Priya hadn't just accepted feedback—**she was now part of the brew.**

Lesson learned: Just as bold coffee needs a splash of milk, feedback needs the right approach to be palatable.

The Leadership Challenge — "I Don't Have Time for This"

Leaders, too, pushed back. Senior manager **Vikram** was blunt:

"Weekly check-ins? I don't have time. Deadlines are looming, and this feels like micromanagement."

Arjun countered with a simple question:

"What if a few minutes now could save hours of rework later?"

Skeptical but curious, Vikram agreed to try. Within weeks, his team made fewer errors, and speed actually increased.

"Alright," he admitted, *"I get it. A quick conversation today prevents a crisis tomorrow."*

Brewing a Culture of Continuous Feedback — The Perfect Blend

To turn feedback into habit rather than ceremony, Arjun launched three initiatives:

1. **Instant Feedback Moments**

   No more waiting for review cycles. Teams shared quick feedback over coffee chats, Slack, or post-meeting de-briefs.

2. **The 3C Feedback Model**
   - **Clear** — Direct, specific, and actionable.
   - **Constructive** — Framed to help, not criticise.
   - **Continuous** — Offered in real time, not stockpiled.

3. *Mini-Example:*

   Instead of *"Your presentation was weak,"* say:

   *"Your slides lack data to back the story **(Clear)**. Adding last-quarter metrics will make them persuasive **(Constructive)**. Let's polish them before tomorrow's client pitch **(Continuous)**."*

4. **Recognition-First Approach**

   Feedback began by spotlighting what worked well, making the conversation energising rather than draining.

Within six months the impact was unmistakable:
- Employee-engagement scores rose **35 per cent**.
- Work quality improved across departments.
- Turnover fell as employees felt supported in their development.

One afternoon, Rohan approached Arjun, a grin replacing his earlier worry.

"I never imagined feedback could feel this helpful. I used to dread it; now it's like a perfectly brewed cup of coffee—it lifts me up rather than putting me down."

Arjun clapped him on the shoulder. *"That's the goal. Feedback shouldn't leave a bitter aftertaste. It should push you forward—one sip at a time."*

Final Reflections — Feedback, Like Coffee, Is Best When Fresh

That evening Arjun penned a simple formula in his journal:

Frequent + Constructive + Two-Way = Growth & Retention

Because Arjun knew—**like coffee, the best feedback isn't just fresh. It's shared often, served warm, and brewed with care.**

Chapter 6
Brewing Tough Conversations

The Bitter Cup of Responsibility

The office tasted different today—thick, heavy, like an over-extracted brew abandoned on the hotplate. The usual hum of keyboards sounded distant, the fluorescent lights sharper. Arjun could feel the dread pooling in the corridors, carried in hushed glances that avoided meeting his. Something was coming—something every HR professional prepares for but secretly hopes never arrives.

Layoffs

The message from the CEO sat in his inbox, subject line as sterile as a sealed envelope of bad news. The numbers were final. A restructuring was unavoidable, revenue curves pointed the wrong way, and good, hard-working people would have to leave. Arjun's throat tightened as he read. In the margins of spreadsheets, every cell equalled a human story.

Internal Flinch

He closed the laptop and pressed his palms to the cool desk. *Is this why I joined HR?* he wondered, eyes stinging. *I signed up to build careers, not dismantle them.* For a heartbeat he imagined walking out, choosing an easier profession. The moment passed—but its aftertaste lingered, dark as chicory.

The Human Side of Hard Decisions

In the HR war-room Ravi was waiting, fingers steepled in thought. Today the mentor's warmth carried extra weight.

"You knew this would happen someday, didn't you?"

He slid a printed list across the table.

Arjun scanned the names—people with mortgages, college-going children, music lessons on Saturdays. "Knowing and doing are different things," he muttered.

"That's why we have to do it right." Ravi leaned back. "Layoffs aren't about delivering bad news. They're about dignity. You need the right *blend*—of empathy and professionalism."

Arjun managed a tight smile; the italics felt appropriate.

The Conversations That Change Everything

Flashback Roast

On the corridor wall hung a photo from six months earlier: Sandeep's team celebrating a product launch, paper cups raised in mock champagne. The memory hit Arjun like the scent of fresh grounds—joyful, bright, now painfully distant.

Sandeep was first on today's schedule.

The engineer entered with a casual "What's up?", unaware that the floor beneath was about to shift.

Arjun steadied his voice. "Sandeep, this is a difficult conversation. Due to restructuring, your role is being made redundant."

Silence bloomed between them. Sandeep's smile evaporated. "Are you serious?"

"It's not performance-related," Arjun said. "You've been outstanding. That's what makes this harder."

The dialogue continued—honest, unscripted, raw. Sandeep's shoulders eventually slumped in reluctant acceptance. "Thanks for not sugar-coating it," he whispered before leaving with a severance packet and teary-eyed dignity.

Lesson 1: Delivering tough news isn't about avoiding pain—it's about standing with people while they feel it.

The Aftertaste – What Happens to Those Who Stay

With the conversations concluded, the office grew quieter, the coffee machine suddenly too loud. Survivor's guilt seeped in like cold air under a door.

During an informal catch-up, Priya, senior developer, cupped a steaming mug but stared past it.

"I still have a job," she said, half-smiling. "But every time I glance at Sandeep's empty chair I think—why not me?"

Arjun listened; silence served as creamer thickening the moment.

She wasn't alone. Over the week he heard:

"It feels like a battle zone—we're the ones left behind."

"I keep waiting for the next list."

The sting of layoffs, Arjun learned, lingers long after the last exit interview.

Rebuilding Trust – Brewing Stability One Conversation at a Time

He convened leadership and outlined a three-phase recovery plan.

1. **Coffee Circle Sessions** – Weekly, cross-functional micro-gatherings—no agenda, no hierarchy. People vented, cried, even laughed. One developer confessed, "I didn't realise how heavy it was until I said it out loud."

2. **Acknowledging the Invisible Load** – Managers trained to swap *"What's your ETA?"* with *"How are you holding up?"*. Productivity metrics temporarily took a back seat to pulse checks.

3. **Digital Tribute Wall** – A bold, contested idea—some executives worried it might "glorify departures." But Ravi backed Arjun. Messages poured in, transforming grief into gratitude. Sandeep's tribute read: *"Your code taught me precision; your jokes taught me patience. You've left a mark."*

To launch these initiatives Arjun drafted a concise company-wide email:

Subject: Brewing Resilience—Together

Team,

The last few days have been bitter. Let's acknowledge that and rebuild our blend of trust and purpose. Starting this week you'll see Coffee Circles on your calendar, resources for emotional support, and a Tribute Wall to honour colleagues who helped shape us.

Let's pour compassion into every cup we share.

— Arjun, People & Culture

Final Reflection: Beyond the Brew

Weeks later, conversations returned; tentative smiles warmed hallways. At the entrance Arjun met **Meera**, a junior HR associate balancing two takeaway cups.

"Morning, Meera," he said, trading one cup for the other.

She looked weary. "Do you ever get used to this part of the job?"

Arjun shook his head. "No. And I hope I never do." He scribbled in his journal:

> *In every bitter brew, there lies a chance to stir in resilience. HR's job isn't just to deliver difficulty; it's to rekindle hope.*

As he sipped, the coffee didn't taste bitter.

It tasted human — like a brew balanced with care, compassion, and the courage to face tomorrow.

Revised Lessons from Arjun's Journey

- Layoffs aren't just about job cuts—they're about dignity and rebuilding trust.
- Empathy and honesty transform difficult conversations into meaningful ones.
- HR's role spans every phase—onboarding, farewell, and the silent spaces in between.
- Survivors carry an invisible burden—acknowledge it, lighten it.

- Supporting those who leave and reconnecting with those who remain are equally essential to cultural recovery.

Self-Written Quote

"HR is like coffee—sometimes strong, sometimes bitter, but always essential. And when it cools, you reheat it with care."

Self-Written Formula

Empathy + Integrity + Aftercare = Sustainable People Practices

Chapter 7

HR Technology–Work Smarter, Not Harder

Brewing Efficiency Without
Losing the Human Touch

The steam from Arjun's coffee curled upward, dissolving into the soft hum of a Monday morning. He stared at his screen; his inbox already overflowed. Somewhere in the chaos of unread emails, overlapping interviews, and policy approvals, he'd lost sight of why he chose HR in the first place.

HR, he believed, should feel warm—like the first sip of fresh-brewed coffee. Yet here he was, drowning in bitter administrative grounds:

- CVs stacked like half-finished thoughts.

- Interview schedules collided—like espresso shots misfired in a chaotic café.

- Employee records buried in spreadsheets, outdated and untouched.

Something had to change.

The Tech Failure That Left a Bitter Aftertaste

The turning point arrived wrapped in optimism—a high-profile recruitment drive meant to showcase HR's efficiency.

Arjun's team had just installed a cutting-edge, AI-powered ATS. It promised speed, precision, and smarter hiring—the espresso shot to power their process.

That morning everything seemed on time. Until it wasn't.

By noon, confusion brewed at the front desk. A candidate stood awkwardly, fingers clutched around her CV.

"Excuse me, I have an interview today," she whispered, "but they can't find my name."

Arjun opened the ATS expecting a quick fix. *Nothing.* The system had rejected her application.

A quick scan revealed why: she hadn't used a required keyword. Not because she lacked the skill—she used different phrasing. **The AI hadn't recognized synonyms; it hunted for exact matches, not intent.**

Before he could act, another HR exec rushed over. "We have a bigger problem."

Two final-round applicants were double-booked for the same slot. One, a senior developer, checked his watch and shook his head.

"If this is how they handle interviews, I'm not sure I want to work here."

He left without a word.

Arjun's stomach twisted. That walkout wasn't a scheduling mishap—it was a trust meltdown.

Moments later an email arrived:

Subject: Lost Candidate – ATS Error Arjun, we just lost our top-choice developer. The ATS rejected her. I saw her resume too late. Another company made an offer. This is a mess.

His coffee had gone cold, mirroring the confidence he had brewed.

Leadership Pushback – "Is HR Tech Even Worth It?"

Later that week, Arjun sat across from sceptical executives.

"We invested heavily in that system," the COO frowned. "And we're losing candidates."

"Maybe we should return to spreadsheets," the CFO muttered. "At least we knew what was happening."

Arjun met each complaint **not with excuses, but with quiet conviction.** He didn't defend the system—he advocated for a smarter way to use it.

"We don't need less technology," he said. "We need thoughtful oversight. Tech should enable human judgment, not replace it."

The CEO tapped the table. "Fine. Fix it. Prove HR tech can work."

Challenge accepted.

Finding the Right Brew: Smart Tech with Human Touch

That night, alone in the office, Arjun stared at a sticky note from his mentor:

> *Technology doesn't brew culture—people do.*

He promised himself, his team, and his company: he would refine the tech like a roaster chasing the perfect roast.

The New Recipe: Brewing Better with Balance

What changed?

- **Let AI filter CVs—but let humans judge the edge cases.** Any ambiguous rejection triggered manual review.

- **Let systems suggest schedules—but let recruiters decide.** Automation set options; people confirmed.

- **Let analytics spot bottlenecks—but let teams choose solutions.** Data illuminated, discussion decided.

- **Let surveys gather signals—but let conversations shape culture.** Online pulses complemented monthly in-person check-ins.

The Turnaround – The Brew That Hit Just Right

At the next hiring drive, everything changed.

Candidates received personalised updates.

The ATS highlighted a quiet gem—no textbook keywords, but grit, clarity, and an impressive GitHub. She was hired and became the team's MVP within months.

Double bookings vanished. The HR team, once buried in digital clutter, found time to hear stories—not just screen CVs.

Full Circle – A Message That Mattered

One afternoon, Arjun's inbox chimed:

Meera: "Thank you for fixing this, Arjun. I didn't realise how disconnected I'd become. Now I actually get to talk to candidates again. It reminds me why I chose HR."

Arjun leaned back, smiling. The tech hadn't just made them faster; it made them more *human*.

Lessons from Arjun's Journey – Brewing Tech the Right Way

1. HR tech is a tool—not a replacement for human wisdom.

2. Automation without oversight is like burnt coffee—costly and hard to swallow.

3. Data should inform and guide decisions, not dictate them.

4. When tech handles process, HR can focus on people.

Final Reflection – Blending Code and Connection

Arjun scribbled in his notebook:

Technology brings efficiency to HR, but empathy makes it irreplaceable.

Automation + Human Oversight + Empathy = People-Centric HR

HR isn't about sipping coffee; **it's about brewing connection**—one line of code, one conversation, one moment of care at a time.

Chapter 8

The Cost of Poor HR–Compliance and Risk Management
Brewing Compliance and Risk Management

From Sipping Coffee to Brewing Trust

Arjun had always believed that HR decisions shaped lives as much as they shaped careers. But it wasn't until a single, avoidable mistake at Aditya Solutions unraveled into a reputational nightmare that he truly understood the weight of that belief.

HR wasn't just about hiring, training, or engagement.

It was about safeguarding.

It was about foresight.

It was about trust—that silent ingredient that made everything else work.

And like the perfect cup of coffee, a single bitter drop of negligence could taint the entire brew.

The Mistake That Burned Deeper Than Expected

It began like any other morning.

Arjun had just poured himself a hot cup of filter coffee when the door to his office flew open. Neha, the bright junior HR associate he'd been mentoring, stood at the threshold—her eyes wide with alarm.

"Rajiv just got terminated," she blurted out. "And… he's furious. He's threatening legal action."

The coffee halted mid-air.

"What?" Arjun said, setting his cup down carefully. "I didn't sign off on that."

No performance warnings.

No PIP.

No HR involvement.

Just a rash decision by a frustrated manager—lacking process, empathy, or documentation.

By afternoon, whispers swept through the office like wind through dry leaves. Trust evaporated faster than steam from his mug.

"If it could happen to Rajiv," someone muttered during a break, "it could happen to anyone."

A few days later, Arjun's worst fears arrived in his inbox.

Subject: Legal Notice – Wrongful Termination Claim

Rajiv was suing the company.

The Emotional Boil-Over: Arjun's Guilt

That night, Arjun stayed long after the lights had dimmed.

He pulled up Rajiv's HR file. The folder was painfully bare—no reviews, no concerns, no coaching notes. Just one terse line: "Performance not up to standard."

Arjun slumped in his chair. His father's words echoed in his mind:

"When in doubt, take a pause—gather facts before you pour."

He glanced at the coffee beside him. It was cold now. Bitter.

Just like Rajiv's last day.

He couldn't shake the image of Rajiv's face. Shocked. Hurt. Betrayed. A team player who had celebrated office wins over coffee and stayed late without complaint—discarded like a misfiled document.

The failure wasn't just procedural. It was personal.

HR was meant to stand between impulsive decisions and human consequences. But this time, Arjun had been too late.

And the cost wasn't just a legal bill. It was brand damage. Disengagement. Trust slipping quietly out the door.

Brewing a New Culture of Compliance and Fairness

But remorse, Arjun knew, had to be converted into reform—or it would become just another bitter memory.

The next morning, he walked into the HR war room with quiet intensity in his gaze.

"No more informal terminations," he said. "No more undocumented grievances. We're putting guardrails in place—not just to protect the business, but to safeguard our people."

Silence filled the room.

Neha finally spoke, "It wasn't your fault, sir."

Arjun shook his head. "If HR doesn't prevent such decisions before they occur… then what is our purpose?"

Reinforcing Documentation

Performance Journals: Managers were now required to record conversations and track progress.

PIPs with Purpose: Struggling employees were given structure—not sudden exits.

Take Meera, for example—a junior developer once at risk of termination. Instead of being cut loose, she received:
- Clearly defined improvement areas
- Weekly one-on-one coaching
- A dedicated mentor

In four months, Meera transformed into one of the most dependable team members.

The lesson? Structured care turns potential exits into success stories.

Strengthening Legal and Ethical Safety Nets

- **Mandatory Compliance Workshops** – attendance required, no exceptions.
- **Termination Oversight Committee** – created to stop impulsive decisions before they harmed lives and reputations.

When Leadership Resisted

Change, of course, never brewed easily.

One afternoon, the CFO stormed into the HR floor.

"Arjun, we don't have time for all this policy fluff. We're a business, not a courtroom."

Arjun stood firm. "We didn't have time to handle Rajiv either—and we paid the price."

The CFO scoffed. "You're slowing us down."

"No," Arjun replied calmly. "I'm protecting what we've built."

Just then, the CEO stepped in. "Let him finish," he said. Then he turned to Arjun.

"What's the cost of rushing to another termination?"

Arjun answered without blinking. "More than just legal bills. It's the erosion of trust—one untracked dismissal at a time."

Silence lingered. Then the CEO nodded. "Let's do this right."

The Trust Shift: From Red Tape to Respect

Not everyone embraced the changes at first.

Some managers rolled their eyes during the workshops. Others muttered about "red tape."

But slowly, the culture began to shift.
- Workplace disputes declined.
- Employee anxiety eased.
- Managers began seeking HR's input—not as a hurdle, but as a safeguard.

Over a quiet evening cup of tea, a senior team lead leaned toward Arjun and said,

"I used to think compliance was about control. But it's really about clarity. People trust us more now."

Arjun smiled. The warmth had returned—not just to his cup, but to the office itself.

Lessons from Arjun's Journey – Brewing Trust Through Compliance

1. **Compliance isn't red tape—it's the invisible thread that holds trust together.**
2. **Documented decisions safeguard both individuals and the organisation.**
3. **Fairness isn't optional—it's a cultural cornerstone.**
4. **HR's greatest strength lies in preventing silent damage before it becomes irreversible.**

Final Reflection – The Guardian Brew

That night, Arjun opened the soft-bound journal where he'd tracked lessons over the years.

He scribbled a fresh insight:

"HR isn't just about hiring or engagement. It's about safeguarding the silent contracts of trust between employee and organisation."

Then, underneath, he added a formula:

Fairness + Transparency + Documented Compliance = Unshakeable Trust

As he closed the notebook, his eyes drifted to a photo of his team. They were laughing—unaware of all the risks quietly navigated on their behalf.

That's what HR really was.

It was never about sipping coffee. Nor about checklists or policies alone.

It was about **brewing peace of mind**, one principled decision at a time.

Chapter 9

Retention–The Secret Weapon for Profitability
Brewing a Culture of Commitment

Arjun cradled a half-empty mug, eyes fixed on the retention dashboard. The steam that once signalled fresh ideas now felt like smoke from a fire he couldn't ignore.

- **Employee turnover** had jumped **30 %** in six months.
- **High performers** were walking out faster than recruiters could walk in.
- Exit interviews echoed one theme: **disconnection.**

Retention, he realised, wasn't a line item; it was a pulse—and it was fading.

The Unexpected Wake-Up Call

The ache became real in the dusky parking lot.

"Heading out late?" Arjun asked, the security lights flickering overhead.

Sandeep, a senior data analyst, rubbed tired eyes. "Half my team's already gone," he said, trying to force a smile.

"That'll settle once the new packages land, right?" Arjun ventured.

Sandeep's laugh was hollow, the clang of his car door cutting through the night air.

"I doubt it. I'm next, Arjun. I don't see a future here— and I'm not alone."

Taillights dissolved into the darkness, leaving Arjun with the biting scent of exhaust and a realisation deeper than any metric: people weren't quitting jobs; they were quitting *us*.

The First Attempt: A Quick Fix That Failed

Panicked, leadership reached for the easiest levers.

1. **Salary bumps** and retention bonuses.
2. **Extra perks**—free lunches, gym passes, permanent WFH Fridays.
3. A mandate to **"boost engagement"** via more meetings.

For three months the graphs looked better. Then resignations spiked—higher than before.

"Pay is fine, but I still don't belong."

"Perks won't feed ambition."

"My manager talks deadlines, never dreams."

Quick wins, Arjun admitted, taste sweet—but they don't satisfy.

Brewing the Real Solution: A Culture of Commitment

Instead of adding cream and sugar, Arjun decided to change the **bean**.

1. **Career Growth, Served Hot**

    - Personalised **roadmaps** for every employee.
    - **Leadership-development** cohorts.
    - A friction-free **internal mobility** portal.

Meenal, a mid-level engineer on the verge of quitting, stayed—her mentor sketched a path she could taste.

2. **Real-Time Recognition: Freshly Ground Feedback**

    - Managers trained to give instant, specific praise.
    - A peer-to-peer kudos app.
    - Strength-first performance reviews.

"A simple 'thank-you' brewed more energy than a double espresso," a sales exec confessed.

3. **A Culture of Listening: Pour-Over Conversations**

    - **Quarterly check-ins** replaced dusty annual surveys.
    - *Coffee Chats with Leadership*—open mic, open calendar.
    - **A stay-interview** program to spot simmering risks early.

"I walked in ready to resign. I walked out feeling heard," said a marketing specialist.

4. **Work That Matters: Flavor You Can Feel**

    - Storytelling sessions linking **code commits to customer smiles.**
    - **Team votes** on product decisions.
    - **Passion-project Fridays**—10 % time for problems employees choose.

"Seeing my design live for users turned my job into a craft," a product designer beamed.

The Impact: Aroma of Success

Six months later, the aroma in the cafeteria had changed.

During an all-hands, a senior engineer raised a cup:

"I was packing boxes six months ago. Now? I'm pouring ideas into something bigger."

Arjun exhaled. Retention isn't about trapping talent—it's about *infusing* meaning.

Lessons From the Brew

1. **Purpose over perks.**
2. **Careers over jobs.**
3. **Daily appreciation beats annual applause.**
4. **Culture is the cup—fill it wisely.**

Retention Formula:

Growth + Recognition + Purpose = ✦ Long-Term Commitment

Final Reflection: Brewing Futures

That evening Arjun closed his journal. Coffee in hand, he smiled.

HR, he now knew, isn't about sipping. It's about brewing careers—one engaged employee, one rich cup, at a time.

Chapter 10

Work-Life Balance–Brewing Happiness Beyond the Office

From Sipping Coffee to Brewing Fulfilment

Arjun stared at his screen while the coffee beside him cooled into a bitter puddle of unmet intentions. Emails, meeting invites, and unfinished reports merged into one long drip—each drop louder than the last.

He wasn't burnt-out yet, but the flame licked close.

The Reality of a Balancing Act

For six years Arjun had commuted between two cities: work in Hyderabad, life in Bangalore with his wife, daughters, and mother. Friday nights meant airport lounges; Monday dawns meant fluorescent lights. He **never** missed a meeting or deadline—yet every weekend blurred into recovery, and airports tasted like reheated espresso.

One Sunday, his younger daughter whispered, "Do you really have to go again, Papa?" As the plane ascended, Arjun's coffee tasted of compromise.

The Employee Struggle – Is Work-Life Balance a Myth?

Determined to gauge the true temperature, Arjun launched a confidential survey:

- **72 %** felt guilty taking breaks.
- **64 %** worked beyond official hours at least three times a week.
- **58 %** said their mental health was fraying under pressure.

One comment stung: *"My children joke that my laptop is my real child."*

The office felt like a **pot of over-brewed coffee—strong, bitter, and hard to swallow.**

The First Failed Attempt – When Policy Fell Short

Aditya Solutions rolled out a **"No Work After 6 PM"** rule:
- Emails disabled after hours.
- Slack silent on weekends.
- Everyone encouraged to leave on time.

Within a month it backfired:
- Work simply shifted to late-night shadows.

- Parents felt judged for needing flexibility.
- Employees left early while managers stayed—guilt steeped deeper.

"I don't need a rule to tell me when to stop. I need a culture that lets me breathe."

Policies without empathy are like caffeine without water—ineffective and unsustainable.

Brewing a Culture of Well-Being

Arjun pivoted from rules to **trust**:

1. **Hybrid Work, Done Right**

   Results trumped hours. Teams set core windows; the rest flexed. Leaders modelled it.

2. **Normalising Breaks**

   Coffee chats encouraged. "Mental Reset Days" approved—no questions asked.

3. **Leading by Example**

   Managers logged off on time; weekend emails became rare, urgent exceptions.

4. **Mental Health as a Business Priority**

   Therapy sessions, well-being check-ins, and burnout workshops became routine.

Laughter slowly returned—like fresh grounds hitting hot water.

The Personal Brew – Choosing His Own Balance

Yet Arjun still lived from suitcase to suitcase. One Sunday night his older daughter handed him a handmade card: a drawing of her debate trophy—and a tiny figure with a suitcase outside the door.

Inside she'd written: *"First prize, Papa… Maybe next time you'll be in the front row."*

Arjun closed his suitcase, opened his laptop, and cancelled Monday's calendar.

> "Tomorrow," he emailed the leadership team, "I'll attend something more important than a Zoom call—my daughter's assembly. We talk about balance; it's time I brew some myself."

In choosing presence over protocol, Arjun realised leadership wasn't about being seen in every meeting—it was about being felt where it mattered most.

The next day, applause filled the auditorium. His daughter scanned the crowd; their eyes met. She beamed. Arjun waved—coffee warm, heart fuller.

Colleagues later whispered, "It meant a lot. Balance isn't policy—it's personal."

A sticky note appeared on Arjun's whiteboard: *"Lead the way you want your people to live."*

Lessons from Arjun's Journey – Brewing a Balanced Life
1. Balance is a mindset modelled by leadership.
2. **Energy managed outranks hours logged.**
3. **Trust, not control, fuels performance.**
4. **Great workplaces support life, not just work.**
5. **True leadership chooses presence**—at work *and* home.

Final Reflection – Work Hard, Live Fully

That evening Arjun boarded a mid-week flight to Bangalore, inbox at peace. In his journal he wrote:

> "Balance isn't about stepping away from success; it's about defining it on your own terms."

And as he sipped filter coffee with his daughter curled beside him, **Arjun finally tasted balance.**

Chapter 11

HR's Seat at the Table–Becoming a Business Partner
Brewing Strategic Influence

From Sipping Coffee to Brewing Leadership

The boardroom hummed like a machine after its third espresso—fast, sharp, and slightly bitter. Slide after slide flashed across the screen—revenue projections, market expansions, competitive strategy—yet none carried the taste of people. With every click, Arjun felt another heartbeat skipped, each line of numbers a reminder that HR's flavor wasn't even on the menu. His coffee cup warmed his hands; its steam fogged the edge of his glasses, but the heat he felt came from something fiercer: impatience.

HR, once again, was at the sidelines.

Not dismissed, but disregarded.

Appreciated, but never essential.

It was as if he'd been asked to sweeten the corporate cappuccino—pleasant, yet peripheral.

Arjun didn't want to sweeten the discussion.

He wanted to **shape** it.

What if HR weren't sugar? he wondered. *What if it were the espresso shot—the bold element that infuses clarity and purpose into every brew?*

The Boardroom Pressure – Every Sip Counts

That day, stakes ran higher than the crema in his cup.

The CEO leaned forward. "Our next challenge is profitability. We need cost reductions and growth—fast."

The CFO added, "One immediate lever is a hiring freeze. We're bleeding budget on a headcount that doesn't guarantee output."

Each word felt like ice dropped into hot coffee—cooling innovation before it could percolate. Arjun's grip tightened, matching the pressure of the beans inside an espresso portafilter just before extraction.

A hiring freeze? That was like removing caffeine from a midnight strategy session and still expecting razor-sharp focus.

"I disagree," Arjun said, surprising even himself with the edge in his voice.

Heads turned. Silence settled like crema atop an untouched espresso.

HR rarely pushed back in this room.

The COO arched an eyebrow. "Arjun, with all due respect, this is about numbers. HR isn't the engine of profitability."

Arjun set his cup upon the table—deliberately, like a barista tapping the portafilter. **"Then let's talk numbers."**

Micro-Story 1: The Product Delay That Cost Millions

He flipped to the first slide. "Last Q2, our time-to-fill sat at 52 days—nearly double the industry average. Development ran short-staffed, delaying the product launch by four months. Lost revenue?" He paused. **"$3.5 million."**

He clicked again. "After we fine-tuned our recruitment grind, time-to-fill dropped to 30 days. The next launch brewed on schedule, generating **$5 million** more."

A hiss of steam seemed to rise as the temperature in the room shifted.

Micro-Story 2: The Sales Resignation Spiral

"Recall when our top sales manager walked out—no development plan, no succession pipeline. She took three key clients with her."

Quarterly revenue in her region fell **15 percent**. Replacement and relationship-rebuilding cost another **$400 k.**

"But once we launched our *Career Growth Pathways*, early attrition cooled by **45 percent**. Replacement spend dropped **$600 k.**"

"Retention isn't just froth," Arjun concluded. "It's the caffeine shot that preserves revenue."

Micro-Story 3: Engagement That Out-performed Expectations

"Remember the customer experience team that exceeded targets three quarters straight?"

He revealed the figures:
- **+18 %** Customer-Satisfaction
- **+22 %** Upsells
- **$2.4 million** in new business

"All brewed from targeted engagement, skip-level dialogues, and peer recognition—ingredients finer than any policy alone."

The Pushback – One Final Brew

The CEO leaned back, contemplative. "You've made your point."

The CFO nodded. "This is the first time I've tasted HR through a profitability lens."

The COO, however, drummed his fingers. "Fine stories, but strategy is about predictability. Can you guarantee future returns?"

Arjun smiled—like a barista confident in the next pour. He revealed a projection dashboard.

"By extending these initiatives to onboarding, we forecast an **18 percent ROI within two quarters**, with a confidence interval of 90 percent. Consistency is our espresso machine—same pressure, same heat, every shot."

He advanced to the final slide.

Arjun's Business Brew

Brew Step	Formula	Impact
Beans	Right people + targeted growth	↗ Market agility
Grind	Retention + development	↘ Cost, ↗ Returns
Extraction	Culture + performance	↗ Revenue acceleration

"**Innovation fuels this company,**" Arjun said, "but *people* fuel innovation. Our job is to calibrate the grind, pressure, and temperature—then pull a consistent shot, every time."

He didn't just present data.

He told stories.

He created **aroma** and **impact**.

The Espresso-Shot Moment: Seat Earned

The CEO closed his notebook. "From today, HR sits at this table for every strategic decision."

Arjun exhaled—not from relief, but from resolve. The crema had settled; the flavor was unmistakable.

The Aftermath – HR, Re-imagined

- HR joined merger discussions **before** term sheets were drafted.
- New business units mapped talent needs **proactively**—not retroactively.
- HR dashboards appeared beside financial KPIs at every board review.

One morning in the pantry, the CFO handed Arjun a coffee.

"You were right," she said. "I thought HR was a flavor. Turns out, it's the kick."

Arjun inhaled the aroma and smiled.

Lessons from the Brew

1. **Measure HR by business outcomes**, not just HR metrics.
2. **People strategy accelerates growth** faster than any cost cut.
3. **Numbers lend credibility; stories make them unforgettable.**
4. **HR doesn't wait for a seat; it *brews* one**—shot by shot.

Final Reflection – The Taste of Influence

That night, Arjun returned to his journal.

"HR becomes indispensable," he wrote, "when it stops sweetening policy and starts pulling bold shots of purpose, people, and performance."

He snapped the journal shut, savoring one last sip.

Because now he knew:

HR wasn't just about **sipping** coffee.

It was about **brewing** leadership—one perfectly extracted espresso at a time.

Chapter 12

Beyond Management–Brewing a Legacy of Leadership

From Burnt Coffee to Brewing Leaders

Arjun remembered the worst coffee he ever had—burnt, rushed, and utterly flavorless. He didn't know it then, but that bitter cup mirrored a kind of leadership he would later reject: reactive, impersonal, and void of care.

A great leader, like a great brew, isn't made overnight. It takes patience, the right blend of qualities, and ongoing refinement. For Arjun, leadership had never been just a position—it was a purpose.

As he climbed the ranks in HR, mastering recruitment, talent management, and performance systems, he realised something profound: Leadership wasn't about titles or authority—it was about impact. And just like the perfect cup, it was about sustaining warmth, depth, and richness over time.

The Awakening: From Recruitment to Inspiration

Arjun vividly remembered his first major recruitment drive—a rapid scale-up to hire 150 engineers in just three months. Initially, he focused on numbers, deadlines, and speed—like a barista rushing through orders without tasting the brew.

Then he met Priya.

Her résumé was impressive, but it was her story that struck him: She had overcome immense personal hardship, excelled academically through sheer resilience, and wasn't just seeking a job—she was searching for purpose.

Something shifted in Arjun. Recruitment wasn't about filling roles; it was about brewing opportunities for people's dreams.

Inspired by Priya, he changed his approach entirely.

"Let's not just fill vacancies. Let's understand stories, aspirations, and align them with our vision."

The result? Roles were filled faster. Retention soared. Morale bloomed. Employees felt valued from the first interaction—like a perfectly brewed coffee leaves a lasting impression from the first sip.

The Mentorship Moment: Brewing Potential into Leadership

One defining moment of Arjun's journey came with Rahul, a talented marketing associate full of ideas but shackled by self-doubt.

Rahul was sharp and diligent, but his voice wavered during presentations. His notes were filled with crossed-out sentences, and he often glanced around, unsure if he belonged in the room.

One evening, after a tough feedback session, Arjun found Rahul alone at the coffee machine, stirring his cup absently.

"You're putting in the effort, Rahul. But do you believe in your own ideas?" Arjun asked.

Rahul avoided eye contact. "I just... I mean, I had an idea, but wasn't sure if it was... you know, worth sharing."

The words struck a painful chord in Arjun. He remembered feeling invisible in school, overlooked and underestimated.

In that moment, Arjun made a decision.

"Let's change that. I'll mentor you personally."

He introduced Rahul to storytelling techniques, helped him lead smaller meetings to build confidence, and made sure Rahul's voice was heard in leadership discussions.

Months later, Rahul stood before the executive team, delivering a pitch that secured a major client. He walked up to Arjun afterward and said, "I finally feel like I belong here."

Leadership, Arjun realised, wasn't about directing—it was about unlocking hidden potential.

The Challenge: When a Protégé Becomes a Challenger

Just as Arjun felt confident in his mentoring, a test arrived.

A leadership role opened in marketing. Rahul was a strong contender, but Arjun hesitated. Was Rahul seasoned enough? Could he handle the pressure?

Before Arjun voiced his doubts, Rahul confronted him.

"Why am I not being considered for this role, Arjun?"

Arjun was stunned.

"I've done everything you taught me. I've taken risks, built confidence, delivered results. But now, when it's time to step up, you're hesitating. Why?"

To complicate matters, Mr Kapoor, a senior executive, weighed in. "Rahul's young. We need someone seasoned. His leadership under pressure is untested. We can't take risks with this role."

That night, Arjun sat alone with his journal, a quiet cup of coffee by his side.

A great leader doesn't just develop others—they let them lead.

The Crisis: A Leadership Test Under Fire

Before Arjun could advocate for Rahul, a crisis struck. A high-stakes product launch was failing. The marketing team was misaligned, chaotic.

The CEO demanded a fix.

Arjun turned to Rahul. "You wanted a chance to lead? Here it is."

Rahul hesitated, the weight of responsibility pressing on his shoulders. At first, he struggled. Team members resisted. Meetings were disjointed.

Mr Kapoor observed with a smug shake of his head. "Told you so."

But then something shifted. Rahul stayed late, listened deeply, and recalibrated the team's strategy. He led from the front, balancing urgency with empathy.

The launch succeeded. The company exceeded revenue targets by $8 million.

The next morning, Arjun handed Rahul the promotion letter.

"You earned this."

Rahul didn't just smile. He said, "I'll make you proud."

Arjun realised: True leadership isn't just about shaping careers. It's about shaping legacies.

Lessons from Arjun's Journey – Brewing a Legacy of Leaders

- **Lesson 1:** Leadership isn't about authority—it's about unlocking potential.

- **Lesson 2:** A great leader doesn't just mentor—they step aside when the time is right.

- **Lesson 3:** Growth happens when leaders create more leaders, not followers.

- **Lesson 4:** Leadership isn't measured by titles, but by the legacies we leave behind.

Final Reflection: Brewing a Legacy of Leaders

Late one evening, reflecting in his journal, Arjun wrote:

Leadership transcends mere management—it's about awakening possibility in every person we meet. Our legacy isn't just defined by the achievements we accumulate, but by the leaders we inspire, nurture, and empower to carry the torch forward.

As he set down his pen, he smiled. Because true leadership isn't about power—it's about impact.

HR wasn't just about sipping coffee—it was about brewing leaders, one inspired individual at a time.

Chapter 13

Brewing Collaboration–Conflict Resolution in Product Engineering

From Sipping Coffee to Brewing Unity

Arjun cradled his mug, inhaling the rich aroma that usually signalled another energetic day. Yet today, the office hum sounded hollow. Between polite greetings lay a silence thick enough to taste—like coffee left too long on the burner.

A **quiet divide** had formed between the *founding engineers*, proud custodians of every line of legacy code, and the *new hires*, brimming with fresh ideas but locked out of the vault of tribal knowledge. Just as over-ground beans brew into bitterness, poorly shared expertise had begun to sour team spirit.

The Silent Rift

Sreenivas, a senior engineer, finally voiced the unspoken:

"Why hand them everything? We learned the hard way. They can too."

The words echoed fear—*If I give away my secrets, what's left of my worth?* New engineers like Karthik, meanwhile, replayed a quieter refrain: *I can't help if I don't know.*

Inefficiencies spiked, code reviews dragged, and innovation stalled. Arjun knew the brew needed a new recipe.

HR Intervention: Four Fresh Brews of Collaboration

"Great coffee needs patience, the right grind, and a gentle pour." — Arjun's favourite barista mantra

1. **Mentor-Mentee Pairings with a Twist** *Mechanism* – Each veteran paired with a newcomer, but mentorship flowed *both* ways. Seniors offered history; juniors shared new tools and trends. *Turning Point* – When Sreenivas's mentee Karthik proposed a concise refactor that shaved hours off a build, Sreenivas felt pride, not threat.

2. **"Brewing Knowledge" Coffee Workshops** Informal circles over cappuccinos replaced dry trainings. Stories of past bugs, triumphs, and near-misses bubbled freely. **Result** – Within three months, participation soared 60 %, and employee surveys showed a 40 % jump in perceived alignment with the product vision.

3. **The Living Product Wiki** A shared, ever-evolving knowledge base captured lessons in real time. **Impact** – Code-review turnaround fell 25 %, and onboarding time

dropped 40 % as new hires navigated context-rich pages instead of stale PDFs.

4. **Leadership in the Limelight** Arjun enlisted execs to *celebrate* knowledge sharers in all-hands. Recognition became cultural currency.

Symbolic Shift – Ravi, once the staunchest skeptic, volunteered to lead a wiki deep-dive, confessing, "I used to guard knowledge like a secret blend. Now I see it should be on tap for everyone."

Anecdote: A Sprint Saved by Shared Knowledge

During a critical release, a mysterious memory leak threatened to derail the sprint. Panic simmered—until Karthik dug into the new wiki and unearthed a three-year-old workaround chronicled by Ravi. The team patched the issue in minutes. Gratitude flowed stronger than espresso, proving shared knowledge beats siloed expertise every time.

The Aroma of Change

Weeks later, the office buzz returned—this time vibrant. Original engineers felt *elevated*, not eclipsed; newcomers felt *trusted*, not tested. Code merged faster, and brainstorming sessions crackled with cross-pollinated ideas.

At the next engineering all-hands, Ravi raised his cup:

"I once thought knowledge was power. Turns out *shared* knowledge is a super-power."

Smiles—and clinks of porcelain—followed.

Lessons Brewed

1. **Insecurity Breeds Hoarding** – Protecting status by guarding knowledge ultimately drains team energy.

2. **Collaboration Is a Culture, Not a Checkbox** – HR must brew trust, not merely schedule trainings.

3. **Two-Way Mentorship Scales Faster** – Fresh eyes plus seasoned minds create the perfect blend.

4. **Celebrate the Sharers** – Public praise converts sharing from extra work into badge of honour.

Formula for Sustainable Collaboration

Ingredient	Result
Shared Knowledge + Trust	Stronger Teams
Open Conversations + Leadership Support	Lasting Change
Documentation + Active Mentorship	Scalable Growth

Final Reflection

As Arjun closed his notebook, he took one last sip. The product was no longer brewed by a select few—it was a communal pot, refilled and refined by all. The best teams, he realised, aren't built merely on experience; they're built on **collaboration**.

Chapter 14

Brewing Future Leaders–Succession Planning and Career Growth

From Sipping Coffee to Brewing Leadership

Arjun stood by his office window, sipping his coffee as the sun cast a golden hue over the city below. As morning light filled the room, he reflected on the journey so far—the company's growth, the challenges overcome, and most importantly, the people who had made it possible.

But with progress came a new challenge: how to ensure the company would thrive well into the future. How could its culture, values, and momentum be sustained? Succession planning wasn't just about replacing leaders—it was about cultivating them. Leadership wasn't a job title; it was a mindset.

Just as a coffee shop can't rely on one blend for long-term success, a business can't depend on a few key individuals forever. It needs a rich, evolving mix of future leaders, ready to step in and stir things up.

The Challenge: Identifying Future Leaders in Engineering

Arjun had spent years with the product engineering team, immersed in its innovation and energy. Yet one question kept him awake: Who will lead this team five years from now?

He saw potential in many engineers—their creativity, discipline, and drive. But few saw themselves as leaders. They loved building. They didn't always picture themselves guiding others. And leadership, Arjun believed, wasn't about barking orders. It was about inspiring, deciding, guiding.

Like a barista selecting the right beans for a new signature brew, spotting leadership potential required patience, intuition, and a willingness to explore unexpected flavors.

The HR Intervention: Brewing Leadership Opportunities

To help this potential flourish, Arjun knew he needed a tailored, human-centered approach. Succession planning had to be personal—as personalized as a hand-crafted cup.

He launched the Leadership Discovery Programme, aimed at finding high-potential engineers, regardless of title, and preparing them for future leadership. The programme focused on both immediate action and long-term growth:

1. **Mentorship Pairing:** Promising engineers were paired with executive mentors who modeled strategic thinking, decision-making, and people leadership.

2. **Skill Development Workshops:** Practical, hands-on workshops helped participants master team leadership, conflict resolution, and product vision alignment.

3. **Cross-Department Collaboration:** Participants led cross-functional projects to gain a holistic view of the business, understanding how product, sales, and support intersected.

4. **Personalised Career Growth Paths:** For engineers close to a leadership transition, Arjun co-designed individual growth journeys, balancing their technical depth with emerging leadership needs.

The First Test: Nurturing a Future Leader in Engineering

One such engineer was Rajesh—quiet, meticulous, and respected for his consistent brilliance. He'd been with the company for five years and had earned admiration through skill, not volume.

When Arjun invited him to lead a cross-functional team, Rajesh hesitated.

"I've always been a builder," he said. "I'm not sure I'm cut out to be a captain."

Arjun smiled. "Leadership isn't about knowing everything. It's about helping others ask the right questions."

Encouraged, Rajesh accepted. His first assignment? Leading engineers and designers in revamping a core product feature. For the first time, his focus shifted from writing code to orchestrating collaboration.

The Unexpected Spill – Leadership's First Bitter Note

Three weeks in, the team missed a major sprint milestone. Designers were frustrated over vague specifications. A junior engineer had twice pushed faulty code into production. Friction was rising.

When Arjun checked in, he found Rajesh slumped in the cafeteria, coffee cold, sandwich untouched.

"I thought I had this," Rajesh murmured. "But I lost control. The team's frustrated. Honestly, so am I."

"Tell me what happened," Arjun asked gently.

"I assumed they'd self-manage—like I did. But I didn't follow up. I let one person dominate. I wanted to be liked more than I wanted to lead."

Arjun nodded, feeling the sting of remembered mistakes. "Rajesh, you brewed the coffee, but forgot to stir it."

Rajesh blinked. "Meaning?"

"You had the right ingredients. But leadership's about blending, not just gathering. Managing the heat, guiding the flavor. This isn't failure. It's your first stir."

The Comeback Blend – Strength Through Support

With Arjun's mentorship, Rajesh regrouped.

He called a team huddle—not to assign blame, but to listen. He clarified expectations, invited quieter voices to speak, and gave teammates small wins to own. He rehearsed tough conversations—Arjun played the role of a grumpy stakeholder over mock coffees.

Soon, the team rebounded. The next sprint was on time and delivered a breakthrough improvement. Internal teams took notice.

At the demo, Rajesh stood tall. His voice, once unsure, was steady. He looked around not for approval, but connection.

Later, Arjun found a sachet of spiced coffee on his desk with a note:

> "Still learning to brew. But now I know it's okay to spill—as long as you stir again." —Rajesh

The Balance: Developing Skills While Meeting Organisational Needs

As Arjun continued nurturing leaders, one truth became clear: growth isn't linear. It isn't titles or promotions. It's fire, stumbles, second brews.

Succession planning wasn't just about building leaders. It was about blending technical mastery with vision.

1. **Technical Mastery Meets Leadership Development:** Rajesh and others stayed hands-on in tech while growing as people leaders. This blend preserved product focus while expanding business perspective.

2. **Long-Term Vision with Immediate Impact:** Leadership prep wasn't future-only. Projects addressed real-time challenges, making development purposeful and tangible.

The Outcome: Brewing Strong Future Leaders

Months later, Rajesh mentored a new aspiring leader. He still coded, but also coached. His team respected him not for perfection, but for presence.

Like a barista who once scorched a batch and now tastes with care, Rajesh infused trust and clarity into every interaction.

Arjun looked around and saw a legacy forming—leaders crafted with empathy and attention.

Lessons from Arjun's Journey

- Succession planning should be personal and patient.
- Leadership isn't a straight path—it stumbles, spills, and recovers.

- Technical excellence and leadership are not trade-offs.
- Supporting mistakes is essential to shaping leaders.
- Growth is a slow pour—built on trust, timing, and consistency.

Final Reflection: Brewing Leaders for Tomorrow

That evening, Arjun sipped cardamom coffee and watched a younger leader mentoring their team. There was laughter. Calm. Ownership.

In his notebook, he wrote:

"We don't just brew leadership. We roast, spill, and stir it until it's ready to serve."

HR, he realized, wasn't just about readiness plans. It was about resilience rituals—creating safe spaces to fail, learn, and rise.

And as the aroma of mentorship filled the air, Arjun smiled.

Some brews take longer. But those are the ones that linger the longest.

Chapter 15

The Final Promotion—Becoming CHRO

From Sipping Coffee to Brewing Legacies

An Email That Changed the Aroma

Arjun's pulse quickened when an unexpected email landed in his inbox on a chilly Monday morning.

Subject: *Congratulations on Your Promotion — Chief Human Resources Officer.* For a heartbeat, time froze. The familiar aroma of freshly brewed coffee from the breakroom, the soft clatter of keyboards, the rhythmic hum of office life—all of it blurred into a distant hush.

This was it. The moment he had envisioned countless times. Not merely a career milestone, but the culmination of every lesson, every challenge, every transformation.

He visualised each chapter of his journey: From recruiting fresh graduates to shaping culture. From navigating conflicts to mentoring leaders. From **sipping** coffee in quiet reflection to **brewing** a workplace where people could thrive.

Yet as the excitement percolated, an unwelcome guest crept in—doubt.

The Cold, Bitter Cup of Doubt

That afternoon, Arjun was summoned to a closed-door meeting with the CEO and CFO. The coffee in his hand tasted **cold and slightly bitter**—a stark contrast to the warmth of the morning.

> "Our employee-engagement metrics have slipped," the CFO began. "Exit interviews point to dissatisfaction with leadership accessibility. Some employees feel disconnected from HR."
>
> The CEO leaned forward. "You've earned this promotion, Arjun, but leadership isn't about individual success alone. Are you prepared to guide a department that's losing touch with its people?"

Arjun felt a jolt. HR was his world—how had he missed this?

That night, **sleep eluded him.** He replayed the CEO's challenge, Riya's lingering frustration from earlier hallway conversations, and his own reflection in the dark office window.

Had he become so focused on proving HR's strategic worth that he'd drifted from its human essence?

He set the untouched mug down—its coffee now **cold and bitter as doubt**—and opened his worn journal.

If people don't feel seen, what are we really building?

A Knock at Midnight — The Catalyst

Just then, a soft knock disturbed the stillness. Riya, an ambitious HR associate reminiscent of young Arjun, peeked in.

"Sir, may I?" she asked, hesitant.

He nodded.

"Sir, when I joined HR, I thought it was about making a difference," she confessed. "Lately it feels like… paperwork, compliance, numbers. I want to believe in what we do, but I don't feel connected to people anymore."

Her words landed like a **sharp espresso shot**—quick and awakening. In that instant, clarity brewed.

Brewing a New Blend of Leadership

The next morning, before officially accepting the CHRO role, Arjun called an all-hands HR meeting. No slides. No agenda. Just **warm, grounding coffee** and open conversation.

Standing before his team, he held up the same worn journal that had guided his journey.

"We've worked tirelessly to position HR as a business driver," he began, "but in doing so, we've drifted from our people. HR isn't about policies; it's about moments that shape lives. If people don't feel seen, what are we really brewing?"

Silence. Reflection. Then nods of realisation.

The First Initiatives as CHRO — Recipes in Action

1. **Leadership Drop-Ins**

   Every HR leader will hold weekly open-door coffee sessions. — Micro-Story: On the first Friday, **Priya from Finance** stepped in shyly. By the second cup, she shared an idea that blossomed into a company-wide wellness overhaul.

2. **Career Story-Sharing Workshops**

   Employees will narrate their growth journeys; policies will be shaped from lived experiences. — Micro-Story: **Rahul, a junior developer**, told how early mentorship changed his trajectory—prompting HR to formalise a cross-functional buddy programme.

3. **The HR Reconnection Pledge**

   HR associates will shadow different teams to feel their day-to-day challenges firsthand. — Micro-Story: After shadowing Customer Support, **Ananya** identified a burnout risk, leading to revamped shift rotations.

4. **Employee-Led HR Town Halls**

   Instead of HR giving updates, employees will voice what they need. — *Micro-Story:* In the debut session, a quiet intern suggested flexible learning stipends—sparking a new professional-development budget.

With each initiative, Arjun felt the department's pulse quicken—like **rich, aromatic coffee swirling in freshly warmed cups.**

A Desk of Reminders

On Day One as CHRO, Arjun entered his expansive new office. He placed three items on the polished desk:

- A **faded family photograph**—a reminder of roots and sacrifices.

- His **worn journal**—inked with lessons, doubts, and epiphanies.

- A **framed diploma**—his first HR-leadership certification, proof of relentless learning.

(Visual suggestion: The camera pans from rising coffee steam to the open city skyline, symbolising micro-to-macro leadership vision.)

That afternoon, he brought the HR team together once more.

"Our role is to **empower voices, shape experiences, and inspire innovation.** Policies manage people; genuine care motivates them. Let's build a culture that everyone aspires to belong to."

These words weren't rhetoric—they were a pledge.

Final Reflection — The Perfect Brew

Long after the office emptied, Arjun stood by the floor-to-ceiling windows. The city lights flickered like dreams in mid-brew. He opened his journal:

> "Leading HR means championing humanity within business. Listen deeply, act wisely, and empower consistently. Let empathy guide your evidence, and integrity shape your leadership."

He distilled his leadership formula:

Empathy + Strategic Vision + Continuous Learning = Sustainable Success

He closed the journal and lifted a **freshly poured, smooth cappuccino**—its aroma bold, its steam curling upward like possibility.

This was it— not the end of a journey, but the beginning of a legacy.

HR isn't just about drinking coffee—it's about brewing legacies, one inspired career at a time.

Chapter 16

The Future of Profitable HR–Brewing Beyond the Present

From Sipping Coffee to Brewing the Future

The city below shimmered with life, its lights dancing like fireflies against the velvet sky. Arjun stood by the window, fingers curled around a warm cup of coffee – not just watching the skyline, but truly seeing it.

Each light wasn't merely a bulb. It was someone's late-night hustle, a battle against burnout, a new idea waiting to percolate. And for the first time in years, Arjun allowed himself to pause – not to strategise, not to fix – but to reflect.

He traced his journey:
- From the dusty lanes of his village where his first job application was handwritten.
- To fluorescent-lit nights spent decoding labour laws.

- To boardrooms where business and people strategy once stood worlds apart.

He had come a long way. Not by sprinting, but by brewing change – one thoughtful cup at a time.

A Legacy in the Making – Enter Rohan

"Sir, got a minute?"

It was Rohan – the young HR executive Arjun had mentored months ago. Anxious eyebrows, yet a spark in his eyes: curiosity steeped in purpose.

"I've been thinking about what you said," Rohan began, brandishing a weather-worn notebook. "About HR being more than policies. I want to build that kind of HR. But sometimes… the future feels too big."

Arjun poured two cups. "The future always feels oversized from the starting line," he said, sliding a mug across. "The trick is to brew it one conversation, one decision, one person at a time."

He turned back to the glittering skyline. "Do you know what the biggest change in HR will be, Rohan?"

Rohan shook his head.

"It will stop being a function and start being the foundation. HR won't live in a department – it will flow through the bloodstream of the business."

Brewing the Future: Not in Theory, but in People

Arjun didn't lecture with slides; he narrated with stories.

When the company needed niche talent in a hyper-competitive market, they had candidates ready before any resignation hit – thanks to predictive analytics. "Think of it like brewing espresso," he said. "You prep before the cup runs dry. That's workforce planning."

He spoke of Priya – the overlooked analyst who flourished under a personalised learning path. "Custom paths are the cafetière of HR," he laughed. "Slow, intentional, rich – never mass-produced."

And during the pandemic, HR stopped being a department and became a lifeline. "Employees didn't need a policy," Arjun recalled. "They needed a voice, a check-in, a 'How are you?' Our new engagement platform wasn't a tool; it was a promise to stay human."

A Bold Brew: The Prediction That Changed Everything

Rohan hesitated. "But won't AI and automation replace a lot of what we do?"

"It will replace tasks," Arjun nodded, taking a contemplative sip. "But not trust. Algorithms might learn roles; only people can build relationships."

"In the next decade, HR won't exist in isolation," he continued. "There will be no 'HR business partners' – only business leaders with people-first thinking. The CHRO won't present reports; they'll co-author strategy. Just as coffee evolved from a morning drink to an experience, HR will become the cultural and economic core of the enterprise."

He let the aroma linger. "But only if we stay human while scaling."

The Three Foundational Brews of Profitable HR

"Let me share the three foundational brews every people-first HR must master," Arjun said, pointing to three hand-drawn icons on the whiteboard.

1. **Predictive Talent Planning** – Brew Before the Cup Runs Dry Arjun recalled the multi-million-dollar deal lost when hiring lagged behind project allocation. "We learned to forecast, not react – to anticipate, not scramble," he explained. "Data, trends, and retention signals keep our pot ready before the customer orders the next round."

2. **Custom Learning Ecosystems** – The Artisan Roast of Growth He gestured to Priya's framed 'Star Innovator' award. "She didn't fit the mould, so we broke the mould," Arjun said. "Learning should be crafted, not cloned – a rich, artisan roast brewed just for you."

3. **Integrated Feedback Platforms** – The Barista Who Knows Your Name Arjun smiled. "Annual reviews were vending-machine coffee – impersonal and stale. We built systems that remember preferences, celebrate small wins,

and ask how people feel, not just what they've done. That's the barista who greets you before you've even ordered."

The Handover – Brewing the Next Chapter

Midnight chimed. Arjun handed Rohan a battered journal – the same one he had carried through boardrooms and breakdowns.

"Every great leader should leave behind recipes, not just results," he said.

Rohan opened to the final page:

"A great brew begins with intent. Choose your beans carefully. Stir with empathy. Let it percolate through listening. Serve it with trust."

Final Reflection – A Legacy Written in Coffee Rings

As Rohan left, Arjun faced the window again.

The skyline hadn't changed – but his role had. No longer merely a builder; now a brewer of brewers. HR, he realised, was never about efficient processes alone. It was – and would always be – about inspiring belief:

- The belief that careers can have meaning.
- The belief that culture can drive profit.
- The belief that even in an AI-run world, the human blend makes the strongest brew.

He took the last sip.

It was rich. Warm. Bittersweet – just like growth. And as the echo of that sip settled in the quiet room, Arjun knew: his job wasn't just to brew answers, but to awaken possibilities.

A Glimpse Ahead: Profitable HR

Arjun slipped a bookmark into the journal's final chapter:

"Coming Soon – Profitable HR: The Business Impact of People Strategy."

The challenges ahead were vast – AI, automation, relentless ROI pressures – but the mission was clear:

To prove that HR doesn't just support business; it drives it.

And that future? It's already brewing.

Conclusion

The aroma of freshly brewed coffee filled Arjun's office as he stood, cup in hand, watching the golden city lights dance against the night sky.

Much like a slowly percolating espresso, his journey had been one of patience, pressure, and transformation.

There were moments of bitterness—challenges that tested his resilience. There were notes of sweetness—small wins that rekindled his purpose. And there was depth—layers of learning, growth, and human connection that made it all worthwhile.

As he took a thoughtful sip, he reflected on how HR had once been viewed as a routine cup of office coffee—efficient, but easily overlooked. But over the years, he had helped turn it into something richer, bolder, and more refined—a brew that fuelled careers, shaped leaders, and transformed businesses.

The Journey That Redefined HR – Brewing Something Bigger

Arjun smiled, tracing the rim of his coffee mug as he turned back the clock to his early days at Aditya Solutions.

Back then, HR was like a lukewarm cup of instant coffee—adequate, but lacking warmth or inspiration.

It was seen as a back-office function, a department that merely hired, processed paperwork, and enforced policies.

But Arjun had never been one to settle for the status quo.

He saw HR as something far greater—a force capable of shaping businesses, empowering individuals, and creating enduring legacies.

He revolutionised hiring, shifting it from a numbers-led process to a mission of discovering potential—like a barista selecting only the finest beans, not just any batch. He transformed performance management into a continuous, two-way conversation—like a slow brew that deepens in richness over time. He adopted technology with foresight, proving that HR wasn't just about people—it was about enabling them through innovation, analytics, and anticipation—just as the right brewing method elevates every cup.

But most importantly, he made HR human again.

He made employees feel seen—like a coffee shop where every regular's order was remembered. He gave careers meaning, ensuring growth was nurtured, not imposed. He built a culture where passion wasn't buried in bureaucracy, but brewed into brilliance—just like a perfectly crafted espresso.

The Moment of Realisation – A Freshly Brewed Perspective

As he sat in his chair, his fingers absently flipping through the worn pages of his journal, Arjun smiled.

Every scribbled note, every ink-stained thought carried the essence of his journey—his insights, his stumbles, his relentless pursuit of something better.

There were days when he questioned the grind—when progress felt bitter and change seemed elusive—but he kept brewing.

HR was no longer just about managing people. It was about enabling them to become their best selves.

He thought about Mira, the once-overlooked employee who rose to become a department leader—like a forgotten coffee blend that becomes a best-seller with the right attention. He remembered Anand, whose quiet contributions might have been lost, if not for the real-time recognition system—much like latte art, precise and thoughtful, elevates the cup. He reflected on Priya, who joined uncertain of her path but found clarity through a personalised learning journey—just as a single-origin coffee, when brewed with care, reveals unexpected depth.

These weren't just HR stories. These were lives transformed.

And that, Arjun realised, was the true legacy of leadership—brewing lasting impact, one career at a time.

The Future of HR—and Beyond

Arjun gazed into the rich swirl of his coffee, knowing this wasn't the end—just the next phase of the blend.

HR had evolved, but its full potential was still steeping—like a new roast waiting to be perfected.

He envisioned HR leaders not as administrators, but as architects of strategy—just like a master barista crafting bold new flavours, not just replicating the old ones. He imagined AI-powered workforce planning, predicting talent needs before they even emerged—as though a barista could anticipate your perfect roast before you placed the order. He saw a future where HR was the bridge between business and humanity—where empathy and innovation weren't at odds, but beautifully balanced—like a cappuccino marrying the depth of espresso with the softness of milk.

HR wasn't a department. It wasn't a title.

It was a movement—one that would continue to brew new possibilities for years to come.

A Call to Action – Brewing the Future, One Career at a Time

Arjun closed his journal, knowing this story was never his alone.

It belonged to every HR leader who ever felt undervalued. Every changemaker who believed there was a better way. Every individual who knew that business must begin—and end—with people.

He left a message on the final page, like the last sip of a perfectly brewed coffee—deeply satisfying, yet hinting at more to come:

"We are not just HR professionals. We are architects of culture, curators of talent, and champions of human potential.

When we invest in people, we don't just grow businesses—we change lives. And that is the greatest return on investment."

Final Reflection – A Brew That Never Ends

As Arjun stepped away from his office that night, he wasn't closing a chapter—he was opening a new one.

HR wasn't just about sipping coffee. It was about brewing careers, cultivating futures, and fuelling what's next.

And with that final, deliberate sip, he savoured not just the taste—

but the promise in every future cup waiting to be brewed.

Acknowledgements

Every journey, much like a **perfectly brewed cup of coffee**, is a blend of experiences, relationships, and moments of inspiration. Writing *A Simple HR Story* has been a **slow brew**—a process of reflection, growth, and immense gratitude. Just as **no great coffee is made with a single ingredient**, this book would not have been possible without the people who have shaped my life, my career, and this journey.

The Beans That Built the Foundation – Family and Early Lessons

To my parents—the very first **roasters** of my journey. Your sacrifices, values and unwavering belief in me have laid the **foundation** for everything I have achieved.

You instilled in me the importance of education, hard work and integrity—the essential elements that turned my raw potential into something meaningful. Your **love has been my anchor, your wisdom my guiding aroma**—infusing every step of my career with purpose and strength. Like the **first sip of coffee on a cold morning**, your presence has always been my **comfort and motivation**.

To my teachers and mentors, from my early school days to my university professors, you were the **baristas** who fine-tuned my thinking, **nurtured my curiosity** and **challenged me to go beyond my limits.**

Each lesson, each **word of encouragement,** and each **moment of constructive feedback** has been like the **right amount of grind-size in my growth—just enough resistance to create a full-bodied result.** You have **taught me that learning is a lifelong process,** and for that I am forever grateful.

The Richness of Support – Family and Balance

To my wife and daughters—you are the **perfect blend of love, strength and inspiration in my life.**

Living between two cities has been like managing the heat of a brewing process—challenging yet rewarding. Your **unwavering patience, love and encouragement** have **kept me grounded and driven.** To my daughters—**your hugs, your endless questions and your pride in me remind me why I do what I do.** Like a **shot of espresso on a long day,** your presence fuels me in ways I can never put into words.

You have taught me more about leadership, patience and balance than any professional experience ever could.

The Perfect Blend – Mentors, Colleagues and the HR Community

To my mentors, colleagues and friends—thank you for being the **seasoned brewers in my career journey.**

Your **guidance, challenges and belief in my vision for HR** have added **depth and richness** to my professional growth. Each **conversation, lesson and shared experience** has shaped my understanding of **what it means to build a people-centric organisation.** You are the flavours that **enhance this brew—bold, insightful and transformative.**

To my team and peers in HR—this book is for all of you who, every single day, **pour your heart and soul into creating workplaces that are not just productive but also human.**

Your **dedication to people-first leadership** is the **crema that tops our profession,** giving it purpose, warmth and undeniable impact. **I hope this book serves as a reminder that HR is not just a function—it's a transformative force, like a perfectly brewed coffee that fuels and energises an entire organisation.**

The Last Sip – To the Readers

To my readers—thank you for picking up this book, for taking this **sip of HR wisdom** and for allowing me to share my story with you.

Whether you are an **HR professional, a leader, or simply someone passionate about people**, I hope these pages resonate with you like a comforting cup of coffee—familiar, energising and thought-provoking. **May this book inspire you to see HR not as paperwork but as the process of brewing lasting careers, shaping strong leaders and creating thriving cultures.**

The Final Pour – A Toast to Everyone Who Believed in Me

Finally, **to every individual who has believed in me, encouraged me and walked alongside me on this journey**—this book exists because of you.

Your **support has been the heat that transforms raw coffee beans into something rich and fulfilling.** Your **insights, challenges and belief in me** have been the **perfect roast that brings out the best flavours in my journey.**

With deep gratitude I raise my cup to you all.

We are not just HR professionals.

We are architects of culture, curators of talent, and champions of human potential.

When we invest in people, we don't just grow businesses—we change lives.

And that is the greatest return on investment—rich, full-bodied and deeply satisfying.

Here's to HR – the art of brewing meaningful careers, one sip at a time.

With deep gratitude,
Sanketh Ramkrishnamurthy

About the Author

Sanketh Ramkrishnamurthy's journey in human resources spans more than two decades, culminating in his current role as Global Head of People Operations at AutoRABIT Renowned for his people-centric leadership style and sharp business acumen, he has spent years aligning talent strategies with business success. His experience cuts across industries – from technology startups to global enterprises – and he is known for blending compassionate people practices with results-driven strategy, earning a reputation as a transformative HR leader.

For Sanketh, leadership is deeply personal. He often recalls sitting with new employees on their first day, eyes wide with hope, and welcoming them like they truly mattered – and later, doing the same on their last day, ensuring they left with dignity. In boardrooms and during tough decisions, he has quietly championed fairness, inclusion, and growth, never shying away from fighting for "the human in the system". This empathy and unwavering commitment to doing what's right define his leadership philosophy and the culture he builds around him.

As a thought leader, Sanketh shares hard-won insights from his career to inspire fellow HR professionals and leaders. He often speaks about resilience – how success and failure are both part of the journey – and champions a growth mindset in the face of change. Whether he's telling the story of an employee triumph or addressing the evolving role of HR in the age of AI, his voice is both pragmatic and heartfelt. His popular LinkedIn posts blend business wisdom with human stories, reflecting his belief that people are at the heart of every great organization.

Those very human moments and lessons are what inspired *A Simple HR Story*. In this book, Sanketh distills decades of experience into an engaging narrative that demystifies HR beyond policies and paperwork. Through relatable stories and candid reflections, he shines a light on the unseen acts of leadership and compassion that keep workplaces thriving. Sanketh's hope is that his storybook will resonate with anyone who has ever led or been part of a team, and spark a deeper appreciation for the "human" in human resources.

Ever the connector and mentor, Sanketh remains active in the HR community. He invites readers to connect with him on LinkedIn to continue the conversation, share insights, or simply say hello – because for him, every connection is an opportunity to learn and uplift others.

Glossary of Terms

- **CHRO:** Chief Human Resources Officer

- **Employee Engagement:** Emotional and psychological commitment employees feel towards their organisation.

- **HR Analytics:** Data-driven approach to managing people at work.

- **Performance Management:** Ongoing process of communication between supervisors and employees.

- **Retention:** Organisational strategies to keep talented employees engaged and committed.

- **Succession Planning:** Identifying and developing future leaders within an organisation.

Call-to-Action

If Arjun's story has inspired you, take the first step towards transforming your own HR practices. Let us continue this conversation together—connect with me online on LinkedIn or via email at sanketh.manas@gmail.com.

IndiePress

The best route your story can take.

To publish your own book, contact us.

We publish poetry collections, short story collections, novellas and novels.

contact@http://indiepress.in/

Instagram- indie_press